# Juniper's Whitening

## and

# Victimese

**Helen Olajumoke Oyeyemi** was born in Nigeria in 1984.
She moved to London when she was four and is currently
studying Social and Political Sciences as an undergraduate
at Cambridge University. Her first novel, *The Icarus Girl*, is
published by Bloomsbury. This is the first publication of her
plays.

T0262467

# Juniper's Whitening

and

# Victimese

**Helen Oyeyemi**

**Methuen Drama**

Published by Methuen Drama 2005

1 3 5 7 9 10 8 6 4 2

First published in 2005 by
Methuen Drama,
A & C Black Publishers Limited
36 Soho Square
London W1D 3QY
www.methuendrama.com

A CIP catalogue record for this book is available from
the British Library

ISBN 978 0 413 77478 1

Typeset by Country Setting, Kingsdown, Kent
Printed and bound in Great Britain by
Cox and Wyman Ltd, Reading, Berkshire

# Contents

# Juniper's Whitening

*Juniper's Whitening* was first performed at the Corpus Playroom, Cambridge, on 27 April 2004. The cast was as follows:

| | |
|---|---|
| **Aleph** | Adam Shindler |
| **Beth** | Gytha Lodge |
| **Juniper** | Katy Burke |

*Directed by*   Helen Oyeyemi, Katy Burke, Gytha Lodge and Adam Shindler

*Out of sight,* **Beth** *and* **Aleph**. *Their voices raised as if in argument.*

**Beth**  So, here it is? My whitening?

**Aleph**  *Our* whitening!

**Beth**  Here's death, and such –

**Aleph**  Such dreams within a demon's dream –

**Beth**  They blossom, thickly, to the touch . . .

**Aleph**  A tree of tongues. A sea of pens –

**Beth**  A forestful of seeking eyes . . .

**Aleph**  Give us pause!

**Beth**  What dreams may come?

**Aleph**  (*halfway through* **Beth**'s *words*)  What dreams may come?

**Aleph** *and* **Beth**  Why do we say we fear to die?

*From* **Aleph** *a deep sigh, and from* **Beth** *choking sounds.*


**One**

*Darkness.*

**Aleph**  Juniper.

*From the corner, a figure (***Juniper***) can be seen creeping across the stage under a blanket.* **Aleph** *stumbles around after the moving shape, flinging his hands out and trying to catch hold of the blanket. He drags the blanket off her, and there is a silhouetted struggle.*

**Aleph**  Just come here a minute! Are you an idiot?

**Juniper**  Leave me alone – just . . . just . . . I'm *serious!*

**Aleph**  You *are* an idiot. What's the matter with you?

**Juniper**  I'll scream! I mean – I . . .

**Aleph**  Will you? Will you scream?

**Juniper** *breaks free, and the lights come on. She is barefoot and messy-haired, dragging the blanket around her and blinking confusedly at the light.* **Aleph** *moves towards her and she retreats, but he only pulls the blanket off her so she's standing in her nightie.*

**Juniper** *indicates the light.*

**Juniper**   Who did that?

**Aleph** *shrugs and drops* **Juniper***'s blanket to the floor.* **Juniper** *now focuses on him.*

**Juniper**   You killed Beth.

**Aleph** *looks at her as if about to explain something, then looks away, hands in pockets, brow creased in frustration, as if he thinks that his theory is too weighty for her.*

**Juniper**   You did it again. You did it again.

*She goes a little closer to him and tries to look into his face, but he backs off and won't give her eye contact.*

Why do you keep on killing her? I can't . . . I mean, it doesn't make sense . . .

**Aleph** *puts his hand out to stop her from trying to touch him, and she freezes.*

**Aleph**   So you were going to run away?

**Juniper**   I saw you. She lay down, and she let you strangle her. You – when she started struggling, you knelt on her – you fucking knelt on her so she couldn't get up –

**Aleph**   I had to; she wanted to.

**Juniper**   Wanted what?

**Aleph**   You were going to run away. I can't believe it.

**Juniper**   What did you expect me to do? I saw you. You're not like that – you're not supposed to be like that.

**Aleph**   What am I like, then? (*Short laugh.*)

**Juniper**   What?

**Aleph**   Why were you going to run away?

**Juniper**   Aleph! Please don't –

**Aleph**   You think I'm going to hurt you.

**Juniper** (*too quickly, almost before he's finished*)   I don't!

*Pause.*

**Aleph**   I was looking for you, anyway. Someone looked out of the attic window today – I could tell from the curtain –

**Juniper**   It wasn't me!

**Aleph** *crosses the room towards her, but she flinches and shies away.*

**Aleph**   Stop being such a wreck – I'm not going to do anything to you.

*He watches* **Juniper** *quickly move forward and pick up her blanket before retreating again.*

**Aleph**   I wondered if you'd seen anyone, heard anyone.

**Juniper**   In the house?

**Aleph**   Well, you don't go anywhere else, do you?

**Juniper**   There's someone else in the house?

**Aleph**   I don't know . . . that's what I'm asking you. (*He looks distractedly over his shoulder.*)

**Juniper**   Will you be able to get her back this time?

**Aleph** *whirls around and starts walking away, peering about distractedly into the next room.* **Juniper** *begins to follow him.*

**Juniper**   *Can* you get Beth back this time?

**Aleph**   Do you really, really care?

**Juniper** (*taken aback*)   What? I . . .

**Aleph**   You're scared of her anyway. You think it really would be better if she just went away.

**Juniper**   Would you shut up?! So suddenly you know what I'm thinking!

**Aleph**   You're so fake, Juniper. It's embarrassing – pitiable.

**Juniper**   You killed her!

**Aleph**   Oh, God! Run away if you want to.

*He disappears into another room.*

**Juniper** *wraps the blanket around herself again.*

**Juniper**   Aleph? Is there really someone else in the house?

**Aleph**   It doesn't matter. You have nowhere else to go.


**Two**

**Beth** *is seated in a chair swathed in blankets, turning a cup over and over in her hands.* **Aleph** *is at her feet, looking anxiously into her face, but she won't meet his eyes.*

**Aleph**   You remember what it is?

**Beth**   Yes.

*A pause. She twists around in her chair so that she's sitting with her legs dangling over the side.*

**Aleph**   What is it, then?

**Beth** *drops the cup on to the floor with a shrug.*

**Beth**   If you don't know what it is, then I'm not going to tell you. (*She stares at the ceiling.*)

**Aleph**   Beth –

**Beth**   It's a cup, a cup, okay?

**Aleph**   I was just trying to –

*He trails off as* **Beth***'s gaze shifts from the ceiling to him. She stares fixedly at him, speaking listlessly.*

**Beth**   What does a cup have to do with anything? What do you mean by it? That because I know what it's supposed to be, that makes me the same as I was before? Is that the logic? Ask me about what you really want to know.

**Aleph**   Beth. You're tired –

**Beth**   You never ask. You never, ever ask. Have you considered that there might have been *cups* where I was last night? Ask me. Ask me! There might have been billions of cups, trillions of them, blooming from trees and bushes, looping down lamp posts –

**Aleph**   Trees and lamp posts, eh?

**Beth**   Yes.

*Beth sits up properly again and, still looking at **Aleph**, she starts to bite at her hand, holding her other hand under it for support. **Aleph** crouches as if to stand, but stays where he is.*

**Beth**   Aleph?

*Enter **Juniper**, gingerly balancing a tray with a messily made sandwich and a glass of milk on it.*

**Aleph** *rises, but doesn't reply, looking instead at **Juniper**, who stands behind **Beth**'s chair, gazing at **Beth**.*

**Beth**   Aleph? It doesn't hurt.

**Juniper**   Welcome back, Beth.

**Beth** *ignores **Juniper** as she first appears and tries to put the tray on **Beth**'s lap, then on the floor, then is eventually relieved of it by **Aleph**.*

**Beth** (*to **Aleph**, laughing*)   Why doesn't it hurt? Why doesn't it?

**Juniper** *takes a seat a little distance away from **Beth** while she's speaking.*

**Juniper**   What doesn't hurt? Beth, what's wrong?

**Beth** (*suddenly angry*)   Aleph! What have you done to me?

**Juniper**   Oh my God, Aleph, what's the matter with her? What's happening?

*She moves towards **Beth**, who has clenched her fists close to her face and is staring over them.*

**Beth**   What is it? What's there? What about the close places? Why have they gone?

**Juniper**   What is she talking about?

**Aleph**   Calm down, both of you – Beth, can we not do this now?

**Beth** *and* **Juniper** (*simultaneously*)   Do this?

**Aleph** *moves away from them and gestures as if to speak, but shrugs helplessly and picks up* **Beth***'s cup instead, putting it on the tray.* **Juniper** *sighs loudly and settles back down into her place, watching them both.*

**Beth**   It doesn't hurt when I bite my hand.

**Aleph**   It's probably just that –

**Juniper**   But did it hurt when he killed you?

**Aleph**   Juniper, you can't –

**Beth**   I can't remember. Yes . . . actually, no.

**Juniper**   No?

**Aleph**   No . . .

*Now leaning on the back of* **Beth***'s chair,* **Aleph** *looks at* **Juniper***, but* **Beth** *turns her face away from them both and closes her eyes.*

**Juniper**   I can't believe you're back. I mean, how . . .?

**Aleph** *is quietly stroking* **Beth***'s back, and neither of them looks at* **Juniper***.*

**Juniper**   I feel as if I'm going mad or something.

*Pause.*

**Beth** (*laughs*)   Can't keep me in my grave – can you, Aleph?

**Aleph**   Maybe we haven't found the right grave for you to belong to yet. Because it's not that I can't keep you there – you just won't stay.

**Beth**   I'd need to be guaranteed certain things before I stayed dead.

**Aleph**    Such as?

**Beth**    Purity. A big, kind pallor. Without it, the end of a life is nothing but a dumb, imperfect cessation of pain – unless a nice person is extinguished, death is silent, confused and small.

**Aleph**    Wow. So you're mocking what you don't have, simply because you don't have it, and if you had it, you'd still mock it, because you don't actually want anything. And you don't understand how it can be that you don't want anything –

**Beth**    You. Are talking. Nonsense.

**Aleph**    No more than you are. Beth, you should be gone; you're still here. Why?

**Beth** *irately clicks her tongue.*

**Juniper**    Beth, did Aleph tell you that he thinks there's someone else in the house?

**Aleph** (*at almost the same time*)    I beg you to shut up, Juniper.

**Beth** *doesn't open her eyes.*

**Beth**    He didn't. But it doesn't matter.

**Aleph** *offers* **Beth** *the sandwich, which she cranes her neck away from with distaste.*

**Juniper**    I'm going to look out of the window. If someone's already come in and done it, then so will I.

**Aleph**    You can't really be that stupid.

**Beth**'s *eyes open. She looks steadily at* **Juniper**.

**Beth**    Yes, Juniper, it's true; don't look out of the window.

**Juniper**    Is that what you did?

**Beth** (*dreamily*)    I wish I were dead.

**Aleph**    So does Juniper.

**Juniper**    Is that what you did, Beth? Did you look?

*She draws close enough to* **Beth** *to touch her knee, then quickly snatches her hand back again.*

**Aleph**   Leave her alone. She needs to eat.

**Beth**   I don't *want* that. I can smell all the things in it; I can smell the wet milk in the cheese, and the sliced animal.

**Aleph**   Sliced animal! It's cooked meat.

**Beth**   There's bleeding all inside it. Inside me, too. I can't eat it.

**Juniper** *reaches for the sandwich on the tray that* **Aleph** *has just discarded.*

**Beth**   I want something small, and light, and crisp. I want . . . little red tomatoes on top of the lightest brown crackers. And no butter; I don't want any. Look at her!

**Juniper** *has just stuffed a large chunk of sandwich into her mouth.*

**Juniper**   I don't care. I'm hungry. There's no more bread! You said you didn't want it, and −

**Aleph** *laughs and helps* **Beth** *up from the chair.*

**Juniper**   Why don't either of you listen to me? You never tell me anything, either.

**Beth**   Will you get me some baby tomatoes, Aleph?

**Aleph**   I will, I'll get them today.

**Juniper**   You need to get some more bread, too, Aleph.

**Beth**   And brown crackers? Will you get me brown crackers?

**Aleph**   Yes, and I won't get any butter.

*Exit* **Beth** *and* **Aleph**.

**Juniper**   It's not fair. I listen to you. I listen to you.

*Exit* **Juniper**.

**Three**

*Dusky half-light.*

**Juniper** *is sprawled on the floor, looking at herself from different angles in a hand-mirror. At the table,* **Aleph** *is carefully placing tomato slices onto crackers. Beside him are a jug of water and three mugs.*

*Enter* **Beth***, carrying a book. She seats herself in the cloth-draped chair positioned behind* **Juniper**. **Juniper** *scrambles up.*

**Juniper**   Sorry. You probably need some rest; I'll just go somewhere else –

**Beth**   If you like.

**Beth** *begins to read, and* **Juniper** *begins to leave, but drops her mirror and bends to pick it up.*

**Beth**   Do you never read?

**Juniper**   Reading hurts my eyes.

**Beth**   What's wrong with your eyes?

**Juniper**   Nothing.

**Beth**   If nothing's wrong with them, then reading wouldn't hurt them.

**Juniper**   I'm disturbing you – I'll just leave and let you . . . read, then.

**Beth**   I'm not reading. I'm talking to you. Don't be scared of me; it's annoying.

**Juniper** *doesn't reply, but backs off awkwardly.* **Aleph** *has stopped moving at the table and is listening, shaking his head every now and again.*

**Beth**   We shouldn't have taken you in, I think. You're not happy.

**Juniper**   But you don't really care about whether I'm happy or not, do you?

**Beth**   Why wouldn't I care?

**Juniper** *looks at her feet.*

**Beth**   I do care. I care about everything. I care about bones, Juniper. Bones don't stay white – they go yellow, and then brown.

**Juniper**   I know. But that's only . . . skeletons, though. And that's got nothing to do with me.

**Beth**   You're wrong. Read this out for me.

**Juniper** *approaches uncertainly, puts the mirror down by* **Beth**'s *chair, and glances at the page that* **Beth** *is holding open.*

**Juniper**   'Nothing lives, that does not die.'

**Juniper** *looks up and catches sight of* **Aleph**, *listening. He smiles at her, but she frowns at him.*

**Beth**   I worry about bones. I wish they changed differently; I wish they whitened instead of darkened.

**Juniper**   Well, *I* can't do anything about it.

**Beth** *shifts in her seat, but doesn't reply, instead looking at* **Juniper** *consideringly.*

**Juniper**   Well, I *can't.*

**Beth**   Don't nursery rhymes drive you mad? They circle in such cruel patterns, over and over, and almost all of them sound eerie sung in the dark.

**Juniper**   I don't know . . . even in the dark, I think nursery rhymes are kind of . . . safe. I mean, what happens when you don't want to think about something? You could start mumbling 'Baa Baa Black Sheep', or you could drown in memories. Pretty simple choice, I think.

**Beth**   Repeating 'Baa Baa Black Sheep' is no way to hang on to your sanity, Juniper. It's that bit 'Have you any wool?' that gives me head-fizzles. Have-you-enny-wool. Gah. I've realised what it is about children that tempts you to murder. They have this littleness to their skulls, and their placid expectancy, like they know it's a rule that they have to be loved – when things are that small and well-formed, you have such a terror of someone or something coming along and bursting them that you suddenly have a crushing strength in your fingers.

**Juniper**  You must have been a child, before. How can you hate them so?

**Juniper** *and* **Beth**  Aleph?

**Aleph** *approaches them with the crackers.* **Beth** *takes one and takes a bite, but then makes a face.*

**Beth**  I don't want these; these are dead, too − they're bland and squishy.

**Aleph**  They probably need butter.

**Beth**  I want water, and I want it to be cool and clean. I want to look into it and see that it's like . . . like a mugful of liquid glass.

**Aleph**  Water? Fine.

*Followed by* **Juniper**, *he goes back to the table and pours water into a mug as* **Beth** *settles back into the chair and closes her eyes.*

**Juniper** (*leaning close to* **Aleph**, *speaking in a low voice*)  Why do you do everything for her?

**Aleph**  Jealous?

**Juniper**  No!

**Aleph**  It wouldn't be nice, having everything done for you?

*He walks back to* **Beth** *with the mug and gets her to sip some water.*

**Beth** (*drowsily*)  Not clean enough.

**Aleph**  I hate her.

**Juniper** *looks at* **Beth** *in alarm, but* **Aleph** *waves a hand dismissively.*

**Aleph**  She's asleep. Look at her. It's wrong to think that pushing your own limits is glamorous, strong. Beth is growing ugly. She goes away, and every time she comes back, another piece has fallen off her. God knows how long she'll be able to hold on to her name, even.

**Juniper**   You don't hate her, Aleph. Why would you keep doing all this if you did?

**Aleph**   It's what she wants.

**Juniper**   But you don't have to do what she wants.

**Aleph**   I was kind to her once.

**Juniper**   Is that supposed to mean something to me?

**Aleph**   Being kind can be a twisted thing. It becomes like a debt you owe to the other one. You cast yourself as decent, and you can't stop.

**Beth** (*eyes still closed*)   He's lying.

**Aleph**   I'm lying.

**Juniper**   I don't believe you!

**Beth**   Who don't you believe?

**Juniper**   I don't know! Leave me alone!

*She walks away from them, and* **Beth** *angrily knocks the mug out of* **Aleph**'s *hands so that the water splashes all over the floor.* **Aleph** *stares at her, but, still staring, moves after* **Juniper** *instead. He and* **Juniper** *talk quietly, she sitting where she's collapsed with her head in her hands, he a little way away from her, kneeling.*

**Aleph**   I thought you wanted us to tell you things?

**Juniper**   I did, but you're making fun of me –

**Aleph** *shakes his head 'no'.*

**Juniper**   And I don't know exactly how. It's because you both know the truth, and . . .

**Aleph**   And?

**Beth** *picks up the mug and creeps closer to them, standing a little way behind* **Aleph**, *clutching it. Neither* **Aleph** *nor* **Juniper** *see her because they are looking intently at each other.*

**Juniper**   And maybe . . . I don't know, maybe you just don't know how to tell it. Or you don't want to, or something. You keep opening up gates so I can run into walls, and I don't know how long I can keep just peeling myself off. It reminds me of the window. I'm not allowed to see outside. It makes me wonder now if there *is* an outside, whether there *is* a window. It's all so exhausting, Aleph.

**Aleph**   Sorry.

**Juniper**   If I wanted to believe that you didn't mean it, I'd say I understand. I'd say I know what it's like when something's happened to you and it sinks and sinks until you can't drag it out again so it sounds real and true.

**Aleph**   Meaning that anything we tell you dressed up as the 'true story' is all discoloured and deformed? Yeah, like it's that simple. Listen to me, Juniper, there is no story. You're inside as far as you can go. You're here just as much as we are.

*He moves closer to her.*

**Juniper**   I'd rather believe the other thing.

**Aleph**   Why?

**Beth**'s *hand, still holding the mug, lifts almost involuntarily as* **Aleph** *moves in to kiss* **Juniper**. *Their lips almost touch.*

**Juniper**   Don't . . .

**Aleph** *touches her face and smoothes her hair.*

**Aleph**   Tell me about what happened to you before you came to us.

**Juniper**   I can't.

**Beth** *sits down so that they're seated in a triangle.*

**Aleph**   Why not?

**Juniper**   I don't know what words I'm supposed to tell it all with.

**Beth**   It doesn't matter – just tell us anything. Tell us about
. . . your mother.

**Juniper**   No. She's mine.

**Beth**   She'll still be yours when you've told us about her.

**Juniper**   No.

**Beth** (*desperately*)   Please? Tell me something real.

**Juniper** *shakes her head emphatically.*

**Beth**   You don't remember, do you? Do you? How can you
not remember?

**Aleph**   Leave it, Beth.

**Beth**   But you know that when things cool I can't leave
them alone. You know. And . . . and . . . you can't take her
away from me! You can never, never, never do it. You don't
have the power. She's nothing to do with you. She's mine.

**Juniper**   I'm not yours! I'm not anything to do with you!
You make me sick. You've crawled out from where the
worms are – I don't want you to touch me.

**Beth**   Then don't touch *him*! He's mine! I'm all over him,
my kisses. You can't take him away from me!

**Aleph** *smiles.*

*Out of sight, something crashes to the floor.*

*All three look at each other, then scatter across the room,* **Juniper**
*scurrying around in panicked circles,* **Aleph** *making as if to leave the
room, and* **Beth** *pacing up and down in straight, steady lines.* **Aleph**
*bumps into* **Beth** *and holds her close for a second.*

**Beth**   What if it's Gimel?

**Aleph**   It's not.

**Beth**   That's what you said before.

**Aleph**   No. You said that.

**Juniper**   Aleph, who is it? What does he want?

**Beth** *puts her arms around* **Aleph** *and lays her head against his shoulder. He hugs her back, while* **Juniper** *wraps her arms around herself.*

**Aleph**   It's no one. No one is actually there.

*Out of sight, a louder thumping noise.*

*A silent pause, then* **Beth** *lets go of* **Aleph** *and claps her hands.*

*The lights come on properly.*

**Beth**   No, you're right. I'm going to bed.

**Juniper** *makes a small gasping sound as* **Aleph** *and* **Beth** *begin to leave.*

**Juniper**   Please don't leave me.

**Aleph**   Then come on; no one's making you stay here.

*Exit* **Aleph**, **Beth** *and* **Juniper**.


**Four**

**Juniper** *is sitting in* **Beth**'s *chair, reading, and* **Aleph** *is at her feet, wearing glasses and writing something down in a notebook.*
**Aleph** *leans over and kisses* **Juniper**'s *ankle, but she shifts her legs and shivers.*

**Juniper**   It happened again last night, didn't it? How can you keep on doing it?

**Aleph**   How can you keep on listening, and doing nothing?

**Juniper**   You know that it's murder.

**Aleph**   Yeah, so I'm a murderer.

**Juniper**   So casual! Is it part of you? It's what you are – like, something you'd put in your passport: occupation – 'murderer'?

**Aleph**   It is, though. But it's not great. It makes me anxious. It's like a task that you dread but has to be done. It moistens my palms and the corners of my eyes, and I grit my teeth until it's over and I'm afraid that they've disintegrated into dust. But you . . . you help, too, from your bed. You help me just by lying there, choking on your own, scared patch of air. You've always heard, haven't you?

**Juniper**  Shut up.

**Aleph**  No. It was only when you saw it happen that you accepted that it was something that you had to handle. Guess what – now you own it! And you're trying to give it back, aren't you?

**Juniper**  What are you talking about? It was never mine in the first place. The . . . guilt isn't mine, none of it is. You don't have to keep killing her!

**Aleph**  And you don't have to stay here. So why do you?

**Juniper**  That's different.

**Aleph**  It's exactly the same thing, and you know it. It all appears voluntary; me . . . being kind to Beth, you staying, but it isn't really. It's like dipping into something smooth and knocking metal – layers, all wrong. We're being forced; and just because it's unseen and only partly felt, you think it's unsafe to acknowledge it.

**Juniper**  Don't tell me what I'm thinking. I can leave when I want to; trust me, I can.

**Aleph**  I told you, didn't I, that when you save someone, there's a warped debt that you owe them?

**Juniper**  I don't remember.

**Aleph**  Don't ever help Beth. Don't do anything that she wants you to.

**Juniper**  She never asks me to do anything. She asks you everything.

**Aleph**  There are lots and lots of different ways of helping. And you do nothing because all three of us know it's a punishment she deserves, and all three of us have to take it.

**Juniper** *pretends not to hear him and turns a page.*

*From another room,* **Beth** *calls out.*

**Beth** (*off*)   Aleph.

**Aleph** *turns back to his writing and says nothing.*

**Beth** (*off*)   Aleph! Where are you? I can't get up.

**Juniper** *begins to stand up, but* **Aleph** *reaches out and grabs her ankle so that she can't.*

**Beth** (*off*)   Aleph?

**Aleph** (*to* **Juniper**)   Shhhhh.

**Beth** (*off*)   Aleph, I want strawberries, as well. Big ones, freshly picked, with droplets of water standing out all over them.

**Aleph**   She's hideous; she's some kind of monster.

**Beth** (*off*)   Aleph? Please? But this is all your fault! (*Crying sounds.*)

**Juniper**   For God's sake, Aleph!

**Aleph**   Don't hear her. Come with me. You don't need to hear her; we can have each other. Come to the window. If you press your face hard enough against the glass, you can't feel anything at all. You become perfect. You mustn't look outside. The safest way is to close your eyes, because then nothing you see inside yourself can hurt you. I promise.

**Juniper** *gets up and hesitantly gives him her hand. He strokes it and starts to lead her away.*

**Beth** (*off*)   I'm sorry, Aleph. Whatever I did, I'm sorry. Please, please, just help me –

**Juniper** *freezes, then breaks* **Aleph**'*s hold.*

**Juniper**   If you don't go to her, I will!

**Aleph**   Juniper, please see. I know I can't make you –

**Beth** (*off*)   ALEPH!

**Aleph** (*to* **Beth**)   You can get up without me. So just do it.

*Silence from* **Beth**.

**Aleph** *lets go of* **Juniper** *and turns back to read over the page he was writing on.* **Juniper** *sits down again, wriggles uncomfortably in her chair and reads a little.*

**Juniper**   Do you think she's okay?

**Aleph** *bends his head closer to the book and doesn't reply.*

**Juniper**   What are you writing?

**Aleph**   A letter.

**Juniper**   In a book?

**Aleph**   It's a letter to myself.

**Juniper**   Oh. What do you have to say to yourself that you couldn't −?

**Aleph**   I could tell you why, if you wanted − I could tell you why you can't leave. But you wouldn't believe me.

*Enter* **Beth**. *She walks unsteadily towards* **Aleph**, *and just when it seems she will crash into him, puts her arms around his shoulders and kisses the top of his head, a gesture that he seems indifferent to.*

**Beth**   Juniper.

**Juniper** *gets up from* **Beth***'s chair.*

**Juniper**   Sorry.

**Beth** *gestures towards* **Juniper***'s book.*

**Beth**   Thought reading hurt your eyes?

**Juniper**   What? Oh. No.

**Beth** *sits down in her chair and looks down at* **Juniper** *and* **Aleph**, *who are now stretched out at her feet.*

**Beth**   By the way, Aleph, it was quite mean of you not to come.

**Aleph**   You managed, didn't you?

**Beth**   It was cruel not to come.

*When there is no response from* **Aleph** *aside from a shrug,* **Beth** *leans forward and beckons* **Juniper** *closer, as if she has something confidential to impart.*

**Beth**   Juniper, I have to tell you something. Don't open cupboards if you fear for your soul. The devil lives in cupboards, and has these bloodshot eyes running along the lines of his shoulders and his fingers, so that they can all look out at you from the shadows in the back. It's nothing but eyes in cupboards, I tell you – even when they're empty. You wonder about what's been happening in them before you open them, and if anything's happening after you've closed them.

**Juniper**   Do you fear for your soul?

**Beth**   Yes, because I have to keep snatching it back from somewhere.

**Juniper**   One day, someone's going to keep it.

**Aleph**   Not if Beth has anything to do with it. She has me holding her to me as soon as the sun rises, saying her name over and over until she can reply to me, and her breathing rips out through her throat as if she's pulling her life from deep in her stomach.

**Juniper**   And you're scared, because every time she takes longer and longer to reply.

**Aleph**   Yes.

**Beth**   Is murder always bad?

**Juniper**   I – what do you think I am, some kind of philosopher? I wouldn't know how to even begin –

**Aleph**   Yes, it is always bad.

**Beth**   Even if you needed to do it?

**Juniper**   What, like self-defence?

**Beth**   Of a sort.

**Aleph**   As in, defence against yourself.

*They consider* **Juniper**, *who self-consciously returns to her book.*

**Beth**   Strawberries, please.

**Aleph**   Will you eat them?

**Beth**   I might. Won't you get them because I might?

**Aleph**   All right. Well, if you don't eat them, I will, anyway. I'm in a mood for strawberries.

**Beth**   Of course you are.

*Exit* **Aleph**, *having scooped up his book and pen with a backward glance at* **Juniper**.

*A few moments' silence as* **Juniper** *returns to her book and* **Beth** *taps the side of the armchair, obviously trying to contain some excitement.*

**Beth**   I saw. I did it!

**Juniper**   What?! Saw what?

**Beth**   I looked out of the window!

**Juniper**   Oh my God! What did you see?

**Beth** *bounces up and down in her seat.*

**Beth**   It was just what I thought it would be.

**Juniper**   What did you see?

**Beth**   I have to kill him, Juniper. It's all wrong because of him.

**Juniper**   Aleph? You want to kill Aleph?

**Beth**   No, no, please don't say 'want to', it's not 'want to' – I have to. I have to kill him.

**Juniper**   Why?

**Beth**   It's because of the bones. The ones that just won't whiten; they make me dirty.

**Juniper**   Beth. For fuck's sake, you can't kill Aleph.

**Beth**   But he can kill me?

**Juniper**   It's not like that; it's not that he's *allowed* –

**Beth**   Tell me, tell me all of it. You're the only good one here. Tell me this – is it true that if you make someone die, and they come out the other side, it doesn't matter? I'm sure *something* clung to Lazarus. Something must've shone through him. It's the bones that don't stay white. Oh, God, you don't understand – I can't let myself become see-through.

**Juniper** *starts forward but then stops short as* **Beth** *curls up in a ball in the chair and rubs her arms as if she's cold, shaking her head as she grows more agitated.*

**Beth**   Every time it happens, I grow stranger to myself. There are pieces and memories that aren't touching any more – it's like a sea-change, except the richness is dark, like soil. I wasn't supposed to change – I wasn't like this before.

**Juniper**   Beth.

**Beth** (*in an undertone*)   Beth. (*She smiles.*)

**Juniper**   Beth? I'm not good. I don't know anything. I feel as if I'm poisoning you both. Something is wrong between you whenever I'm around.

**Beth**   It's not you. I think . . . Aleph and I are supposed to love each other, but we can't. The love is hanging on us like a smell, and we're both fighting it as hard as we can. He hates me, so he kills me.

**Juniper**   But, Beth, you wanted it. You let him – I saw. You can't blame him for not whitening, and you can't blame him for the sea-change. It matters that he makes you die, but . . .

**Beth**   I don't think you know how to finish what you're saying. I wish you could.

**Juniper**   Would it make things better?

**Beth**  Yes.

**Juniper**  Words would make it better? You're telling me your happiness is wrapped up in the right thing said at the right time?

**Beth**  Yes. Little things chiming together, letting you believe for a second that nothing is an accident, and letting you keep that foolish second close to you. I've had too few of those.

**Juniper**  If words can make it better, then I'm sorry.

**Beth**  Stop going on about the words – it's not them, but the feeling I get from them. It's like the window.

**Juniper**  What did you see out of the window? Tell me.

**Beth**  I saw outside. It's daytime, and someone is there.

**Juniper**  Tell me.

**Beth**  No, it's mine.

**Juniper**  Beth –

**Beth**  I'm going to poison him. I have some stuff left. I hid it before – I don't know why. He poisoned me once, of course. Strangling used to hurt me.

**Juniper** *says nothing, but stares at her.*

**Beth**  He is like a toy – an ugly, ugly toy that you only keep because you can wind it up and make it do things. I can tell him what's real, and he believes me because he has no alternative. It's spoiling me in ways you can't see, Juniper. Shhhh. I can hear him. He's coming back.

**Juniper**  Beth, don't do it! Please, don't; promise me you won't – I couldn't handle it –

**Beth**  Shut up, please shut up, PLEASE!

*Enter* **Aleph**, *with strawberries.*

**Beth**  Thank you.

**Aleph**  Can you swallow them okay?

**Beth** *nods, and allows him to feed her a strawberry.*

**Beth**   Mmmm. Much better – not alive, but the juice . . .

**Juniper**   Well, that was quick!

**Aleph**   I didn't know you'd timed me.

**Juniper**   Of course I didn't! It just . . . felt quick!

**Aleph**   Hmmm. What's the matter with you?

**Juniper**   Nothing!

**Aleph** *looks puzzled, then darts a sudden, cautious glance at the area behind him.* **Beth** *rises out of her chair and sits down again, seizing a cushion and holding it to her.* **Juniper** *looks at them both, confused.*

**Beth**   Someone's coming from the attic, someone's treading on the air; they're making it sink.

**Juniper***'s eyes grow large as she begins to feel frightened.*

**Juniper**   Someone else is here.

**Beth**   Someone else is here!

**Juniper**   Who is it?

**Beth**   WHO IS IT? Oh, who is it?

**Aleph** (*helpless*)   I don't know. For God's sake, Beth, calm down.

**Juniper**   Aleph, make him go away. I know who it is; we know who it is, and we don't want him, we don't want him.

**Juniper** *moves towards* **Aleph**, *but he goes and hugs* **Beth**, *who has her arms held out to him, and tenderly kisses her on the forehead.*

### Five

**Juniper** *is lying on her side in bed, eyes wide open as she stares into space, listening. Every now and then, she shivers.*

*Enter* **Beth**, *carrying a lantern, tiptoeing across the room to touch*

**Juniper** *lightly on the shoulder.*

**Juniper**   Ah!

**Beth**   Shut *up*! He'll hear you!

**Juniper**   What do you *want*?

**Beth**   I survived tonight. I thought you might want to celebrate.

**Juniper** *pulls her blankets up around her and edges away from* **Beth**.

**Beth**   Have you been thinking about what I said before? About how he needs to die? Will you help me?

**Juniper**   No! How could you even –

**Beth**   Shhhh!

**Juniper**   Leave me alone, Beth. Just leave me alone. I don't want any part of this.

**Beth**   But . . . you wanted me to share the window.

**Juniper**   Did you see something that told you –?

**Beth**   If you want to know so much, go and look yourself. In fact, I'll take you. Come on.

*They struggle.*

**Juniper**   Don't! I'm scared, all right?

**Beth**   Why?

**Juniper**   I've been thinking about it, worrying about it, fearing it for so long now, that window. It's made you murderous, and God knows what it's done to Aleph – I don't want to change like that; I – I don't want to have to learn a different way to know myself. It's too late for me. I can't do it.

**Beth**   I don't care about all that. You don't even know what you mean. Just help me!

**Juniper**   I can't! I can't stop you, but I can't help you. Let go of me, let go, let GO!

**Beth** *slaps her.*

**Juniper**   It's not that hard. If you really want to do it, all you have to do is put the stuff in his tea. Or if you want to be really creative, bake it into his bread – cyanide bread, y'know.

**Beth**   But poisoning someone is so lonely.

**Juniper** *laughs incredulously.*

**Beth**   I felt like . . . this is silly, but I felt like I had to share it. I couldn't bear to have it all on me. I'm sorry. Never mind.

**Juniper** *tentatively reaches out to touch* **Beth***, and* **Beth** *catches her up in a fierce, tight hug.*

**Juniper**   It's okay, it's okay.

**Beth**   I already did it; it's happened, it's done.

**Juniper** *doesn't seem to hear her.*

*Enter* **Aleph***, with glass of strawberry juice.*

**Aleph**   Everything all right?

**Beth**   Yes.

**Juniper**   Actually, I was thinking of trying to get some sleep –

**Aleph**   Oh, well . . .

*He sits down so that the three of them are in a triangle,* **Juniper** *on the bed,* **Aleph** *and* **Beth** *on the floor.* **Juniper** *snuggles back down into her covers and tries to go back to sleep.*

**Aleph**   What did you juice the strawberries for? I prefer them as fruit.

**Beth**   It *is* still fruit. Anyway, it doesn't matter what you prefer.

**Aleph** *puts the glass down on the floor in front of him and pulls* **Beth** *closer to him so that they are unflinchingly looking each other in the eye.*

**Aleph**  True.

**Beth** *breaks free from him, and* **Aleph** *picks the glass up again.*

**Aleph**  Sure you don't want any?

**Beth** *shakes her head silently.*

**Aleph** *pauses with the glass to his lips, then speaks to* **Juniper**.

**Aleph**  Help me.

*As* **Juniper** *slowly rises from the bed and stares at him open-mouthed, he smiles at her, gives a short laugh, and gulps down the juice.* **Beth** *catches him in her arms as he lets himself fall sideways and starts making rasping sounds.* **Juniper** *leaps out of bed, pushes* **Aleph** *aside and, shouting unintelligibly, starts hitting* **Beth** *over and over as* **Beth** *throws her hands up to protect herself. Eventually,* **Beth** *pushes* **Juniper** *off, and they both look at* **Aleph**, *who has staggered up and fallen into* **Beth***'s chair.*

**Beth**  You have to help me now.

**Juniper** *ignores her and starts putting her shoes on.*

**Beth**  Where are you going?

**Juniper**  Where do you think I'm going?

**Aleph**  Help me.

**Juniper**  Aleph, I can't.

**Beth**  And you can't stop him, either, right?

**Juniper**  You knew.

**Aleph**  Yes.

**Beth** (*to* **Aleph**)  Shut up! (*To* **Juniper**.) We need to put him in the attic.

**Juniper**  I'm going home.

*The chair rocks hard as* **Aleph** *struggles, then dies.*

**Beth**  You don't have a home.

**Juniper**  I'll make one.

**Beth**   Please. Help me take him to the attic, and then you can go wherever you like, and make whatever you like.

**Juniper**   Why the attic?

**Beth**   The window is there.

**Juniper**   Oh . . . oh, my God.

*She helps* **Beth** *lift* **Aleph**, *and they awkwardly carry him away.*


**Six**

**Beth** *and* **Juniper** *are sitting on* **Juniper**'s *bed, with a lamp a short distance away from them.* **Beth**'s *arms are wrapped protectively around* **Juniper** *as she shakes.*

**Beth**   It's all right, it's all right. He won't turn into bones for ages.

**Juniper**   I can't believe.

**Beth**   Believe what?

**Juniper**   It. This.

**Beth**   You don't have to.

**Juniper**   Aleph's dead.

**Beth**   I know.

**Juniper**   I don't want this to be true. I don't want this to have happened.

**Beth** *hugs her tighter, but with a distant expression.*

**Beth**   It was self-defence. Defence from myself.

**Juniper**   I didn't like the way his face was, when the skin was so slack, and it was so easy to close his eyes, as if he were plasticine. I didn't like it, Beth.

**Beth**   Children's skulls are really, really fragile – you can tell by tracing your fingers over them, thinking, testing, pressing.

**Juniper**   *You're* the murderer, not him. You're like some madwoman, wading in a sea of corpses, searching for little stabs of non-colour, flashes of white bone until you're nothing but bones yourself.

**Beth**   Are you scared of me? If you are, let go of me.

**Juniper** *tenses and hesitates, then stays where she is, hugging* **Beth**.

**Beth**   You were scared of Aleph.

**Juniper**   No.

**Beth**   He didn't make sense to you like I do. Can I tell you a story?

**Juniper**   Is it a true one?

**Beth**   No.

**Juniper**   Tell me.

**Beth**   There was a girl who lived in a small house with her parents. She was born in a hospital ten minutes away from her house, and when she was older she went to the school down the road. Her best friend lived next door, and if she'd eventually have had a lover, he would have been the shy boy who lived on the other side of her –

**Juniper**   Didn't she have a lover in the end?

**Beth**   Shhh. Don't spoil it. Both of the girl's parents had to go to work so that they could have enough money. The girl's mother was very pretty, but she never had time to put on any make-up or do her hair nicely, or put on nice clothes. It made her cross, and sometimes she'd tell the girl off for no reason. And the girl's father was very busy as well – he worked in an office, and brought lots of papers home all the time, and it made him very stressed. But he always said he loved the girl –

**Juniper**   Oh my God, Aleph's dead. It's horrible realising it all over again.

**Beth**   Hush, now. Anyway, the girl's parents both said that they loved her very much, but they were lying. The important thing to remember is that danger doesn't lie in the far-away places. It isn't something that soars beyond sight. Tasting is dangerous, touching is dangerous – everything is. You see, it didn't matter that the girl went to school down the road and had her best friend next door and was safe in the close places, because in her house, inside her parents' bedroom, when her mother was still at work, her father would need help to forget all about work and money. And he would tell the little girl to come closer. He wanted to touch her. He'd say –

**Juniper** *struggles away from* **Beth**.

**Juniper**   Stop it! Shut up! No, no, no!

**Beth** *(almost at the same time)*   It was all right, until the girl started having periods. He took her to the doctor's and got her pills, but she'd sometimes forget to take them, of course. So she –

**Juniper** *(hands over her ears, crying)*   No, no, stop it! I don't like the story, I DON'T LIKE IT.

**Beth**   You know the end, I think. You know the end. She had a baby, but it made her mother very angry that she'd had one.

**Juniper**   It's not a true story, though. It's not real.

**Beth**   No, it's not. The girl hurt the baby, because the baby was the thing that made her parents hate her. Things shouldn't be that simple, but they are. The baby was a boy – she called him Gimel.

**Juniper** *has taken her hands away from her ears and is now staring into* **Beth**'s *eyes*.

**Beth**   She started off small; she'd pinch Gimel hard when no one was looking, or she'd drop him on the floor, or she'd make him *need* her – she'd make him cry for ages and ages before she fed him.

**Juniper** *(weakly)*   Please stop.

**Beth** *is crying*.

**Beth**   Then one day, she burnt him. She had hair-tongs, and she got them really hot. She couldn't stop burning him.

She didn't really try to stop. No one else was at home, you see, and they wouldn't be back for hours. When the tongs cooled, she heated them up again, Juniper –

**Juniper**  Oh, God.

**Beth**  Danger isn't far away. She thought Gimel was dead, because he was so still. But he wasn't; Gimel was still alive. Only he looked horrible; he didn't look like a baby any more.

**Juniper**  He did, but he was a patchwork baby, all bruises and scars crossing . . .

**Beth**  You're right. And the girl knew that Gimel would want to take everything from her, and would mark her with his darkness, and his anguish, and his silence. Juniper, Gimel would have killed me simply because the kindness of killing him wasn't in me. Oh, I want to die, I want to die. Oh, please let me.

**Juniper**  Stop asking me! I'm not good! Listen to me, Beth! You know! I'm not good! Listen, it's all right, it's a story, it can be all right, it's your story, you have a chance, I mean, a responsibility, you must weave the story right, you must trace each thread so that it comes out strong and true. Listen, what I mean is, what happened to Gimel?

**Beth**  I don't know. Aleph said he'd take care of it.

**Juniper**  Who is Aleph?

**Beth**  I . . . I don't know. I think he came because I needed him. And then he wouldn't go away. Because it's possible to invite madness, Juniper – it's possible to open your arms wide and hug death.

**Juniper**  What's at the window, Beth? Please tell me.

**Beth**  One. Beth, you just said. Beth. Oh, Juniper. If I can't be dead, I want to be you.

**Juniper**  What? Why?

**Beth**  Because you think you don't know.

**Juniper**  Beth, you're frightening me.

**Beth**   Two. Still, after what I told you? Frightened, why? You're the white, I'm the brown. You shouldn't be scared of what you know. Are freshly buried corpses afraid of their earth? I'm the one who can remember, but you're the one who *knows*. Everything that happens here is because of me, us. Everything happens because we want it to happen.

**Juniper**   Beth –

**Beth**   Three. If you aren't careful, you won't ever die, you know.

*Fade to black.*

**Seven**

**Juniper** *is curled up in her bed, sleeping.*

*Enter* **Aleph**.

**Aleph**   Beth.

**Juniper**   Mmmm.

**Aleph** *kisses her, and she sleepily puts her arms around his neck.*

**Aleph**   All better now?

**Juniper**   Much. Where did you go?

**Aleph**   When?

**Juniper**   Before.

**Aleph**   Nowhere. What do you want for breakfast?

**Juniper**   Strawberries. Big ones, freshly picked, with droplets of water standing out all over them.

**Aleph**   But will you eat them, Beth?

**Juniper**   I might. Won't you get them because I might?

**Aleph**   Then I will. In a minute.

**Aleph** *sits in* **Beth**'s *cloth-covered chair and writes something down, then closes the book with a somewhat wistful expression. Then he begins to leave the room, but is stopped by* **Juniper**.

**Juniper**   Aleph, wait.

*He stops and turns to face her. She recoils as she sees something strange in his face.*

Where's Beth?

**Aleph**   What?

**Juniper**   Aleph. Tell me.

**Aleph**   Beth –

**Juniper**   No!

**Aleph**   But I don't know what you mean!

**Juniper**   Don't lie to me, Aleph! Don't lie to me, or –

**Aleph**   Or you'll kill me?

*Trembling,* **Juniper** *watches* **Aleph** *walk across the room and sit down in* **Beth***'s chair again.*

**Aleph**   That's not a big enough threat any more. There can't be any threats now – I can't believe you don't see that. That's what makes it all so horrible. I'm here because you need me – I'll always be here, for as long as you need me. Juniper's dead. She's finally dead. It was so hard, it was so, so hard – I had to . . . she's all in pieces – she told me to, she made me! She couldn't bear it . . . she . . . you were next, Beth, and I love you . . .

**Juniper**   Don't call me that! I'M NOT BETH! I'M NOT BETH! Do you know what she did? She's so evil. Gimel –

**Aleph**   Beth – you're the winner. You always are.

**Juniper**   No, I've lost. You hate me – you hate her. No – you're dead. We put you by the window . . . the window.

*She runs out of the room, pursued, after a confused delay, by* **Aleph**.

*After a moment's silence, the sound of laughter is heard, followed by glass shattering.*

# Victimese

## Characters

**Eve**
**Toper**
**Ben**
**Megan**, *Eve's sister*

# One

**Eve**   Dark? Hello, dark. This is me. Me? Hello, this is the dark. I am ancient, the springy earth found underfoot in the forest primeval. Pleased to meet you.

**Eve**, *wearing a baggy dress over a skirt, is lying face down on the floor of her cluttered, harshly lit college room, with her hair trailing out all around her. Her room is full of posters and soft toys. The wall above her desk is lined with 'Mr Men' posters. On the ground near her is a closed photo album.*

*There is a knock on her door, and she turns her head so she can speak.*

**Eve**   Yes, come in, why not? Come in, come in, please, hurry up.

*She turns her head back and lies still again just as* **Toper** *opens the door and comes in.*

**Toper**   Hey, Eve.

*She murmurs something indistinctly, then rolls over slowly and holds out her bandaged wrists, meeting his eyes directly, aggressively. The bandages are dappled with blood.*

**Eve**   Look what I did!

**Toper** (*on an outward breath*)   Shit. What happened?

*He comes towards her and gently tries to take her arm, but she slides away from him and crosses the room.*

Are you okay?

**Eve** *shrugs and looks past him, at the door.*

**Toper**   Say something.

**Eve**, *now sitting with her back against the wall, crosses her legs and, eyes on him, slowly begins to unpeel her bandage.*

**Toper**   Eve. Don't do that.

**Eve**   You want me to say something. Fuck you. What do you want me to say? Where have you been all this time?

**Toper**    You look terrible. Did you do that to yourself?

**Eve** *stops unpeeling her bandage, but looks at him coldly before running her hands distractedly through her hair.*

**Eve**    Do not question me. You don't have the right to ask me anything, okay?

**Toper**    You realise that you can't be like this all the time? You can't just hide yourself away and . . . and . . . hurt yourself like this. The others just aren't interested any more. They think . . .

**Eve** (*raising her voice above his*)    You already know I don't care about what they think –

**Toper**    They think you're attention-seeking. They think you're being faux-eccentric.

**Eve**    Yeah? And what do you think? Or are you just going to hide that because you're such a good person? I bet you came to help me. But paying for your help would grate on me.

**Toper**    Pay? What –

**Eve**    Yes, there's a formula – you know what I'm talking about. I'd need to start speaking victimese to you; tell you about how much I'm hurting and how it all seems so hopeless – I'm supposed to honour you with the pretence that you can reach me, that you can actually make a difference to what's happening in my head, and then, when you have these ego-coins in your hand, you'll lavish your help on me. Only it wouldn't really be help at all. Besides, I can't remember the victimese for 'thank you'.

**Toper**    You know what; you're taking the piss. And if I didn't think that you needed someone to be here right now, I'd just leave. I want you to know that. I've been here every day – I've come and knocked on your door every day since you suddenly decided not to bother with any of us any more. Were you even here?

**Eve** *looks at him with an unfocused expression, then stands and walks towards him, then past him, to her chair.*

**Eve**    I was here. (*She draws a circle on the floor with her foot.*) This is where I was. I was fixed right here, for . . . oh, hours, I don't know how many hours. Maybe it was minutes, actually, or maybe it didn't happen at all, but you know what I mean. I was sucked out of my own body – I was an Eve-shaped brick dumped right into the middle of time. I sat and sat, and every time I began to feel I could get up I found out I couldn't; as if the light in this room was thickening into some kind of special glue, made to hold me. I couldn't seem to . . . get away from the light, the strange light in this room.

**Toper** *puts his arm around her and she collapses into him, looking more thoughtful than distraught. He speaks into her hair.*

**Toper**    Eve, I don't think it's the room. I think it's you.

**Eve** *pulls away from him to give him an assessing look, then goes across to her desk and starts pulling posters away from the wall above it.*

**Toper**    Isn't your sister supposed to be staying with you this weekend? Does she know you're not . . .?

**Eve** *is steadily continuing to rip at the posters.*

**Eve**    It's a shame; I suppose you're not the one. You're not rude enough to me. You don't have any courage to lend.

**Toper**    I really did come and knock. I was worried when you didn't answer, so I tried to call you.

**Eve**    No one knocked.

**Toper**    Well, maybe you just blocked it out –

**Eve**    I'm telling you no one knocked. I listened, and listened, I listened right down to the bottom of my hearing, to that bit where you get nothing but a sharp whine. So don't talk to me about blocking things out. No one knocked.

**Toper**    Well, what about your phone? Did that not ring either, then?

**Eve** *kicks the pile of crumpled-up posters she's made into the middle of the room, saving one poster, turning it over and laying it, blank side up, on the floor.*

**Eve**   I didn't want to pick it up. If I had had to speak, I don't know what I would have said.

**Toper**   What are you doing?

**Eve**   Not telling.

**Eve** *starts going through her drawers and eventually pulls out a stack of letters, rummaging in between until she has the full pile.* **Toper** *looks as if he's about to pursue the topic, then abruptly changes his mind and walks over to the pile of posters, sorting through it until he finds the photo album. He opens it and looks at the pictures in silence, then winces, closes the album and puts it back down.*

**Toper**   Why did you take these?

**Eve**   It matters because −?

**Toper**   Eve. I really don't need this. I've had no sleep. When you do things like this, say things like this, it makes you unreal. It makes me feel as if I made you up. I − I'm just really tired. And I haven't even done anything to you.

**Eve**   Except try to help me. How arrogant you are. I don't remember telling you I'm in a place that I don't want to be in. It's the way you assume that being unhappy has no value; like everyone has to crawl and beg their way to happiness. Like only happy people are worth something.

*She scatters the letters on the floor, then kneels down, fetches scissors and starts cutting them up. Toper frustratedly clasps the back of his head and stretches.*

**Toper**   Will you let go of this idea that I'm trying to help you? If you want, *be* unhappy. But I don't trust you not to do something that would make everyone feel guilty.

**Eve**   Like kill myself?

**Toper**   Something like that.

**Eve** (*flatly*)   Go away now.

**Toper**   Okay . . . so those pictures. Did you want me to
see them? Did you leave them there on purpose?

**Eve**   Wounds have faces that tell you things, just like
everything else. I'm not afraid of pictures. I would actually
quite like you to leave now.

**Toper**   Oh, right, I've displeased you. I forgot I'm not
allowed to question what you do in any way.

**Eve**   Haven't you gone yet?

**Toper**   I don't think you're well, Evie.

**Eve** *puts her scissors down and goes to take a Pritt-Stick from her
desk.* **Toper** *hands her the photo album, deliberately letting it flick
open before she catches hold of it, but she seems unfazed.*

**Eve**   I don't think *you're* well. In fact, if I'm ill, it's partly
because of you. You're the worst out of all of us – no self-
awareness. I mean, at least the others can hear themselves
when they speak; at least the others didn't try and create
themselves. I thought you were interesting at first, but
sometimes too much complexity is sickening – it gives you
the baulking feeling of doomed similarity; the same way
brittle things shudder when they catch glass in the act of
splintering.

**Toper**   Yeah, I know you are; but what am I?

**Eve** *pulls a face at him.*

**Toper**   Look – I'm too tired to hear about our faults. The
words are falling right through me. (*Gesturing towards the
letters.*) And are those mine? Are you trying to make some
kind of statement with me standing right here?

**Eve**   It's going to be a collage. It's going to be the ugliest
collage in the world, and it's going on my wall.

**Toper**   Oh, cool. Shall I join in? If you like, I'll get right
down beside you and cut up everything I wrote. It'd be
quite funny, actually.

**Eve** *places the fragments of paper beside each other and tips her head to look at them consideringly.*

**Eve** (*without looking up*)　I want you to admit that you have lied to me a lot.

**Toper**　Okay, so I have. Does that make you feel better?

**Eve**　I want you to tell me why you came here, and why you keep knocking. If you tell me it's because you care, I will bite you.

**Toper** *laughs, but Eve looks at him in silence, smiling a little.*

**Toper**　So you believe I knocked?

**Eve**　Tell me why you knocked, and then go away.

**Toper**　I guess I'm curious. I have a kind of half-theory that you don't really know what people are like until you see their own particular kind of craziness.

**Eve**　Oh . . . like reality's a kind of house that we all concede to share, but everyone has their own private room that they slip into under pressure. You want to walk around, see what things people have slicked on to their walls. Is that what you mean?

**Toper**　No. If we're talking rooms, then we're all in our own private rooms already.

**Eve**　So it's not really that crucial after all. I don't know why you'd bother with other people's psychoses when you've got your own.

**Toper**　Yeah, why not be self-obsessed? You seem really good at that.

**Eve** *reads aloud from the fragments she has lined up in front of her, and* **Toper** *good-humouredly comes up and looks over her shoulder as she reads.*

**Eve**　Believe in me, please.
　　I'm waiting here.
　　I thought of you first.
　　So you can be made safe.

**Toper** (*cringing slightly*)    So you can begin to learn how you'll never die.

**Eve**    Your vein-laced skin, warm with your blood.

**Toper**    Because I dreamed you.

**Eve**    Can you see how beauty makes its shapers into slaves?

**Toper** *backs away, smiling, but clearly unsettled.*

**Toper**    I'm going to go now. I hope you and your sister have fun, if she's still coming.

*He reaches the door, but Eve stands up and speaks quickly, holding out a hand to him.*

**Eve**    Listen. I'm going to tell you this, not because I want help from you, but because it's true, and 'cause you happen to be my best friend. Every now and again, someone, somewhere meets their nemesis, and I just can't shake the feeling that mine's waiting for me.

**Toper**    Well, do you have a message for her in case I see her?

**Eve**    Toper, it's not funny. I'm hiding. I . . . I just don't want to see that face. I'm scared of everyone. I know that whoever it is is close, and that I've been given to them. I'll walk out, maybe to a lecture, maybe even to the frigging canteen, and I'll meet that person who's carrying my death for me, carrying it criss-crossed around the tight skin of their throat as if they have my last minutes in a pouch around their neck. People like that, they're inescapable. Their eyes seem to say: yes, I'm beautiful. And yes, I am going to fuck you up, but not simply because I'm beautiful – that's your fascination; that's incidental in the same way that cruelty glitters when it shouldn't. You know that glass that we're only supposed to see through darkly? When it clears, it'll be stunning, 'cause at the base of it all, we're happy when we perish. When we die, we can finally get some rest.

**Toper** *looks at her with surprise and slowly dawning anger.*

**Eve**    It's up to her to knock, and up to me to let her in.

**Toper**   You actually believe this, don't you? That someone's waiting out there for you.

*An impatient three-rap knock on the door.*

**Eve**   Come in.

**Megan** (*hastily from outside*)   Yeah, it's me!

*Another impatient rap.* **Eve** *rolls her eyes, smears some Pritt-Stick on the back of her hand, considers it, then starts gluing a strip of Toper's love letter to the poster.*

**Megan**   Hello, I'm here!

**Toper**   Come in.

*Enter* **Megan**, *who is wearing jeans, flip-flops, a peasant blouse and three belts criss-crossed over each other. She is jerkily over-confident and has the air of a girl who isn't comfortable in her skin yet.* **Megan** *squeals and runs at* **Eve**, *nearly lifting her into the air as* **Eve** *stays limp in her embrace.*

**Eve** (*sighing with a measure of tolerance*)   Have you finished?

**Megan**   No, I could hug you forever; I'm so glad to see you – sorry I'm early – but I couldn't just *wait around* to be picked up. (*To* **Toper**.)   Are you Eve's friend? Of course, you must be, or you wouldn't be here – hee-hee –

**Toper** *manages to return her smile with one that's more like a grimace and tries to get past* **Megan**, *who is in his way.* **Megan** *continues talking, patting his arm as if speaking to him but really talking over his shoulder to* **Eve**. **Megan** *is looking fixedly at* **Eve**'s *wrists.*

**Megan**   I'm so glad I'm here – I was almost ready to run away from home – nobody understands me there. Half the time, I'm like, flipping hell, why won't you just leave me alone –

**Toper** *smiles with embarrassed relief as he wins the door and begins to leave, but* **Eve** *calls out before he can get out.*

**Eve**   Oh, sorry, by the way, this is Toper.

**Megan**   Hi! We're just about to go and get some food –
God, Eve, I'm starving sooo much – d'you want to come
with us?

**Megan**, *eyes still on* **Eve***'s wrists, turns away from* **Toper** *with a
pointless, nervous giggle that almost spills out of her and stows her bag
in the corner of* **Eve***'s room. Then she goes to the album and starts to
pick it up before it's taken away from her by* **Eve***.*

**Eve**   Actually, I thought we could order in food? Is that
okay?

**Megan**   Well –

**Toper**   I've really got to go. I already said I'd go and eat
with some other people . . . another time? Maybe?

**Eve** (*in tones that say 'no'*)   Maybe.

**Megan**   Oh!

*Exit* **Toper**.

**Megan** *turns and follows* **Eve** *around the room as she gathers up
handfuls of paper and throws them back into her top drawer, then
replaces her glue and scissors and shifts the posters back into the corner.*
**Megan***'s eyes are on* **Eve***'s bandages.*

**Megan**   Are you okay?

**Eve**   Yeah! Of course I am.

**Megan**   Don't really believe you. You seem kind of like
the way I was when I couldn't sleep. It was the worst thing;
I hated to shut my eyes –

**Eve**   Well, I'm sleeping fine.

**Megan**   Who was he? (*Gestures to the door.*)

**Eve**   Toper.

**Megan**   Yeah, but who is he to you?

**Eve** *goes to her telephone and begins to dial.*

**Megan**   He's cute.

**Eve** *puts the phone down and begins dialling another number.*

**Megan**   I don't think he likes me, you know.

**Eve** *peers over her shoulder at* **Megan** *and presses her hand to her heart in mock-sympathy.*

**Megan**   I kept having this weird dream about you. That was why I tried to phone you before. Sorry I woke you up – I had to make sure you were all right. You know, I swear that sometimes dreams are the psychic equivalent of a dig in the ribs – the pain lets you know something's wrong.

**Eve** *puts down the telephone and goes to* **Megan**, *sinking to the floor and pulling her down so that they're lying with their arms interlinked.*

**Eve**   What's the matter?

**Megan**   I wish I knew. It's not just the other stuff I told you about –

**Eve**   Good. Because everything about you is enough. You're pretty enough. You're clever enough. You're enough of yourself to be different. You didn't even need me to tell you that. You know that.

**Megan**   Don't say that; I can't understand you when you're fitting your lips around the words you think you should say.

**Eve**   The dream you had; was it me or you?

**Megan**   It was you. You were . . . laughing. It was just this mad laughing that got to me. And you were alone, laughing underwater, pushing up bubbles so big they bulged like glass fruit. The water looked soupy, brackish, blackish, and you couldn't see me, but I could see you. At first, I was laughing too, but I had this prickling feeling here – (*Brushes fingers down her forearms.*) because I didn't know what we were laughing at, and then I got tired of laughing, but you went on too long. And I didn't know why, and it was scaring me – you know, properly scaring me. Your eyes were wide open, and the whites were pulled tight, like webs of spun metal. And this dream, every night, three times in a row.

**Eve** *lies still with her eyes closed, face turned up towards the ceiling.* **Megan** *gets up on one elbow and looks at her.*

**Megan**   But you're one of those people who're always all right somehow, aren't you? I don't think I ever saw you lose sleep about anything.

**Eve**   I'm not a victim.

**Megan**   Victims lose sleep?

**Eve**   Yeah. They lose everything, because they're not used to winning – how are you going to grab the prize when your fingers have been stamped into a pulp?

**Megan** *tries to prise open* **Eve***'s eyes, but* **Eve** *carefully and easily rolls her out of the way.*

**Megan**   Sis, can you hear yourself? You're saying victims don't sleep.

**Eve**   Are you hungry?

**Eve** *opens her eyes and sits up, and* **Megan** *pauses for a split second.*

**Megan**   Are you?

**Eve**   I asked you first.

**Megan**   Yeah, I know, but are you hungry?

**Eve**   No. But if you are –

**Megan**   No, I'm not either.


**Two**

**Eve** (*whispers*)   It's up to her to knock, and up to me to let her in. I wish I could – oh, please, let me be strong.

*Early morning.* **Eve** *is sitting upright in the middle of her bedroom floor, staring with fascination at the door, chin in hand.* **Megan** *is asleep in* **Eve***'s bed, barely visible under the blanket except for the top of her head. Looking up at* **Megan** *every now and again,* **Eve** *edges* *closer and closer to the door, then finally closes her eyes as if to ready herself and lays her hands against it, bowing her head in an attitude of waiting.*

*The alarm clock goes off, making her jump.* **Megan** *stirs.*

**Megan**    Ah . . . morning!

**Eve** *quickly stands up and starts looking for her jacket. She frowns disapprovingly on noticing that* **Megan** *has slept in her clothes.*

**Eve**    Didn't you bring a shirt to sleep in? And why did you bring an alarm clock into this room? They're not allowed.

**Megan** (*yawning*)    I didn't want to waste too much time sleeping – it always makes me feel a bit guilty to spend hours and hours unaware that I'm alive.

**Eve**    Well, what would you be doing instead?

**Megan** *shrugs.* **Eve** *finds her jacket and puts it on, checking in her pocket for her keys, which she begins to fiddle with.*

**Eve**    Dream much?

**Megan**    No, not at all, thank God. I didn't quite let myself fall asleep. Every time the room started swimming, I pretended someone had this flat in their fist and was shaking it to wake me up. And it worked!

**Eve**    Hm . . . you wanna get breakfast?

**Megan**    Do you?

**Eve**    Do you?

**Megan**    No?

**Eve**    Well, I'm hungry. Will you come to the canteen anyway?

**Megan** (*faux-reluctantly*)    All right.

**Megan** *jumps out of bed and runs to get her coat from her pile in the corner while* **Eve** *moves towards the door, then takes a deep breath before opening it and looking outside. After an uncertain second, she closes it and stands with her back against it.*

**Megan**   I'm ready; let's go.

**Eve**   I think . . . I'm going to have a couple of friends over later.

**Megan**   Okay, cool, let's go.

**Eve**   To celebrate my deathday. Would that be cool; a deathday party?

**Megan** *looks dubious but determined to humour her sister.*

**Megan**   Yeah, good idea. Morbid, but good. It has to be today or tomorrow, though, if you want to have it while I'm here.

**Eve**   Yeah, I know, but it wouldn't be difficult to organise. I'll just call Toper and Ben, and we'll have cake and stuff.

**Megan**   Sounds good. Hey, is Ben cute?

**Eve**   Ben has no face – he's so neutral-looking that everyone assumes he's cute.

**Megan**   So he is cute?

**Eve**   Megan, I don't know. He gets on with most people, as people who never say what they mean tend to do. Yes, cake, and candles, and music, and we'll tell secrets.

**Megan**   And can we have breakfast now?

**Eve**   Yeah . . . I'm not really that hungry after all.

**Megan**   Oh.

**Eve**   Unless you are?

**Megan**   No.

**Eve** *takes her coat off and goes and sits at her desk so that her back is to* **Megan**. **Megan** *stares at her back, bemused, then goes and gingerly sits back down on the bed.*

**Megan**   So what do you want to do today?

**Eve**   I don't really know. I might finish my essay –

**Megan**   Okay!

**Eve** *turns around and pulls an apologetic face.*

**Eve**   Sorry, this must be a boring visit for you.

**Megan**   No, of course not! (*She bites her lip, then loses control and bursts into tears.*) Can you understand how it makes me feel for me to arrive, and then find out you don't want to do anything but have a deathday party? You have this way of going around acting as if everyone else is wasting your life – you must realise that. I know I invited myself over –

**Megan** *puts her head in her hands and dries her face while* **Eve** *stays where she is, writing, with her back to* **Megan**.

**Eve**   Don't keep inviting yourself over, then, if it's going to upset you so much.

**Megan**   But I wouldn't feel as if I had you at all otherwise – you'd just be the girl who swanned in and out of her room at home.

**Eve** (*sharply*)   Stop that.

**Megan**   Stop . . .?

**Eve** *turns and stares at* **Megan** *with hostility.*

**Eve**   Speaking like that.

**Megan**   Sorry?

**Eve**   You're still doing it.

**Megan** *drops her hands from her face and returns* **Eve**'s *stare. Enter* **Ben**, *looking dishevelled and wearing crumpled clothes. He bursts in without knocking, carrying a pillow and blanket.* **Eve** *appears momentarily taken aback, but very quickly recovers herself, and* **Megan** *immediately stands up, then stays awkwardly standing, twisting her hands together.*

**Eve**   Um, good morning . . .

**Ben** *puts down his bedding, and* **Eve** *accepts a kiss on the cheek from him.*

**Ben**  Morning. You look terrible. I'm going to try and get
to sleep in here. You make me uncomfortable, but no more
uncomfortable than that park bench I tried. I was so cold;
even in my dreams I was cold – I was pretty sure I'd die.

**Megan**  Oh, you can't sleep either? Isn't it the most
sickening thing ever? I tend to get this dead feeling in the
space between my eyelid and my eyeball – (*She ineffectually
tries to demonstrate.*) and I start worrying that –

**Ben** *turns to* **Megan** *with an appreciative look, begins to address
her, then realises he doesn't know who she is and, blinking hard,
abruptly stalks over to* **Eve***'s desk, picking up her photo album and
looking through it.*

**Eve**  Ben, this is my sister, Megan.

**Megan**  Hello!

**Ben** (*looking her over*)  Hello. (*To* **Eve**.) I wondered. She looks
like you.

**Eve**  Really?

**Megan**  Thank you!

**Ben**  No, actually I just thought I should say that.

**Ben** *puts the album back down without comment, looks at his pillow
and blanket, then decides to get into* **Eve***'s bed.*

**Eve**  Ben, you might take your shoes off before doing that.

**Ben**  Well, you might've changed the sheets for me.

**Eve**  You seriously can't sleep?

**Megan**  Is it because of a dream?

**Ben**  No. But I bet you can't sleep because of a dream –

**Megan**  Yeah –!

**Ben**  And I'm asking you not to tell me about it, because
I am deeply uninterested in other people's dreams. However –

**Megan** *turns to* **Eve** *in uncertainty, and* **Eve** *quickly puts her arm around her sister and hugs her, then looks across at the album and frowns at it.*

**Ben** (*softly, falling asleep*)   Toper's bringing breakfast around – I hope you don't mind. Sleep and breakfast at the same time is just heaven – I hope it works.

**Eve**   No, that's good. I didn't really feel like going out anyway.

**Ben**   Come into the bed with me, Megaera. Will you?

**Megan**   Okay . . .

**Megan** *laughs loudly but uncertainly and moves closer to* **Eve**, *who has stepped away from her.*

**Eve**   Well, for starters, her name's Megan.

**Ben**   I am so tired. I'm not even making any sense. I haven't seen you for ages, Eve. Are you different inside? Shuffle over here and let me place my fingers in your wounds.

**Eve**   Megan, he doesn't act like this all the time – usually he's the blandest person I know.

**Ben** *sits up and makes exaggerated leering faces at* **Megan**.

**Ben**   Yeah, deprive me of sleep and suddenly I'm a fucking paedophile. How old are you anyway? Fourteen? Fifteen? You're fit, girl.

**Eve** *and* **Ben** *laugh, but* **Eve** *stops when* **Megan** *can only manage a tremulous, outsider's smile.*

**Eve**   Oh . . . come on, Ben, she's my little sister.

**Ben**   'Ben, how could you?' I'm not sorry; I didn't even do anything. Do you know how tired I am? I'm too tired to relax. I start to go to sleep, then I can feel every single part of me buzzing – it makes me feel too alive to fall – I don't dare, in case I shut down completely. God, I can say what I want to her – she fancies me, anyway.

**Megan**   Shut up! Eve, tell him to shut up –

**Ben**  Oooh, tetchy. For a few minutes there it seemed like you wanted my attention, Megan.

**Eve** *sighs as* **Megan** *retreats further away from* **Ben**.

**Eve**  Seriously, leave her alone. You're embarrassing her now.

**Ben**  No, no, I'm asleep, honest. Well, I think I am.

*Enter* **Toper** *after a perfunctory knock, with muffins and a carton of orange juice.* **Ben** *sits up and tuts.*

**Ben**  You call that breakfast?

**Toper**  Bacon would have gotten cold. (*To* **Eve**.) Do you have plates?

**Eve** *sits down abruptly and looks around at them, trying to recall.*

**Eve**  I don't think so.

**Toper**  Well, have a look, will you? I swear you had some at the beginning of term.

**Megan** *smiles* **Toper** *a hello, and he smiles back and hands her the muffins and juice, which she puts on top of the photo album on* **Eve**'s *desk.*

**Eve**  Did you notice this is my room? I think I'd know if I had plates.

**Ben**  Ah . . . you must've smashed them all in one of those eccentric rages of yours. You can tell us, you know.

**Megan** (*laughingly, to* **Eve**)  Eccentric rages?

**Eve**  Oh, go to sleep, Ben.

**Eve** *strides across the room and pushes* **Ben** *back down into the bed. He tries to pull her down into the bed with him, but she slips out of his grasp, wincing as he presses too hard against her bandages. She turns to reseat herself in her desk-chair so she can watch the room, but while she has been fighting Ben,* **Toper** *has taken his seat in the desk-chair, forcing* **Megan**, *who had been edging towards it, awkwardly to bump into him, then turn and perch herself on the edge of* **Eve**'s *other chair, by the door.*

**Toper**   Why don't you pop next door and borrow some plates from Hannah?

**Eve**   We don't need plates – it's only muffins.

**Ben**   Yeah, I actually don't mind drinking juice straight from the carton, or eating muffins out of the packet. But I think your sheets are going to get messed up.

**Toper**   Will you just get the plates?

**Toper** *and* **Eve** *look at each other,* **Eve** *thoughtful.* **Ben** *rolls his eyes and beckons to* **Megan** *to bring a muffin, but when she brings it, he baulks at eating it and starts picking at it somewhat listlessly, his half-closed eyes turned on Eve.*

**Eve**   Megan, would you go and knock on Hannah's door and ask if we can borrow four plates? We'll probably need them for tonight anyway.

**Megan**   Okay! Is Hannah nice?

**Eve** *shrugs, but* **Toper** *speaks before she can reply, directing his comment to* **Eve** *though it's ostensibly to* **Megan**. **Ben** *looks at* **Eve** *and mouths 'Tonight?' in confusion, but she doesn't look at him.*

**Toper**   She's all right. Why don't you do it? Megan doesn't even know Hannah.

**Eve**   Neither do I.

**Megan**   Oh, I don't mind doing it, it's fine – it's always easier asking favours from people you don't know. I'll be back in a second!

*Exit* **Megan**.

**Toper**   I saw an ethereal young woman with the strangest eyes outside. Her eyes . . . they were like frost tipped with light; ice melting with a glow stabbing through it. She had a velvet pouch on a chain around her neck, and she asked me if you were ready to receive her.

*Startled,* **Eve** *moves towards him, then decides to ignore him and takes the chair vacated by* **Megan**.

**Toper**   Does it surprise you that your nemesis would have beautiful eyes? People who are greedy for their own pain, and for the pain of others, would always have very beautiful eyes, eyes to make you hurt.

**Ben**   Oi. Have you gone crazy?

**Eve** *looks at* **Ben** *in silent appeal, but* **Toper** *gets up from the desk-chair and moves so that he is between them and they are forced to break eye contact.*

**Toper** (*to* **Ben**)   No, I just haven't had any sleep. It makes me so angry when I can't sleep – it's the worst between about two and four when the morning colours haven't crashed down on my pupils yet, and I have to try and feel something just so my heart doesn't stop. (*To* **Eve**.) Remember how I like to fit inside other people's psychoses? So I thought about you, and your wretchedness, and your spiteful hiding, and it was all I needed to set me off. The most exquisite eyes are aggressive, unflinching, assessing, aren't they? I know a girl who has those eyes. She tries to undo other people, just because she doesn't know how to be whole. They offer her love, and she despises them for it.

**Eve**   Love? You fucking liar. Those letters weren't even to me.

**Ben** *rolls out of bed and holds* **Eve** *back from hitting* **Toper**.

**Toper**   Right, so if you love, that makes you a liar. And let's look closer at this loving liar – he's a bloated potato-head on a stick, a face to draw smiles on with coloured crayon, a heap of stuffing made to be hollowed out by a foot, kicking.

**Ben**   Children, children, stop this . . .

**Eve**   Tell him that! He's the one who won't shut up.

**Toper** (*circling so that* **Eve** *and* **Ben** *have to swing around*)   So hide here in your room until you feel safe. And you're going to keep your sister here with you too, so you can make her bleed just that little bit more. Well, you're never going to be safe that way.

**Eve** *cuts across him, and* **Ben** *judges from the slump of her shoulders that it's safe to let her go. She steps towards* **Toper**, *who steps back, then sits down hard on the desk-chair.*

**Eve**  Did you see that woman? Is she really there?

**Toper** *looks at her with disgust, then picks up a muffin and starts unwrapping its casing without looking at her or the nonplussed* **Ben**.

*Enter* **Megan**, *cradling plates with cups atop them, to uncomfortable silence. She looks at them all and immediately fails to suppress a nervous giggle.* **Eve** *breathes deeper and shows visible signs of calming.*

**Megan**  Hannah's lovely! I would've invited her around, but I didn't know whether you were good friends with her or not. She says to try not to break the plates. She has this sweet little goldfish that's a kind of bluey silver, and –

*She trails off and blushes as* **Ben** *shoots her a predatory glance from where he is standing by* **Eve**'s *desk.*

**Ben**  Good. So . . . what's happening tonight?

**Megan** *goes to the desk and dumps the muffins on to plates, then realises nobody really wants to eat them and pours herself some orange juice.*

**Eve**  A surprise.

**Ben**  Hate surprises.

**Eve**  A deathday party, then.

**Ben**  Now that's interesting. You intend to kill yourself today?

**Eve**  No; but I never saw the point of birthday parties. And I get the feeling that today is the day I get picked off, that's all.

**Megan**  Oh, don't say things like that!

**Eve**  Well, if I do die, then the party was appropriate – if I don't, then we'll have had cake at least.

**Ben**  Very good. Can it be a deathday gathering for all four of us? Toper, buy some drinks.

**Megan**   Oh, this is going to be fun! I wonder if it makes any difference if you're unable to sleep around other people who can't sleep?

**Eve**   Excuse me, but I'm sleeping fine.

**Toper**   Why don't we just do this thing now? We're all here.

**Megan**   It'll be spookier in the dark, though. Don't you think the night's the best time to feel on the edge of death? You get like that sometimes, that numb, sleepless feeling that spreads until it becomes a wet hand that covers your face. Some polar expiation . . .

**Ben**   Well, I don't get that.

**Megan**   An omen in the bone –

**Ben**   It's just that terrible, taut buzz for me –

**Megan**   – of death's tremendous nearness.

**Ben**   – like an industrial-strength caffeine kick. It seems to affect the way I speak –

**Eve** *smiles with irony at* **Megan**, *who can't find it as funny.*

**Ben** (*to* **Toper**)   And as for you – we know lack of sleep makes you . . . irritable.

**Megan** (*to* **Toper**)   You poor thing! How long has it been?

**Eve**   What are you doing? What are you talking about? Shut up.

**Ben**   What's the matter now?

**Eve**   You're mulling things over, picking your scabs, and any minute now, you're going to start asking each other for help to sleep.

**Toper**   And what's wrong with asking people for help?

**Eve**   Humour me. Pretend I'm a photographer. Pretend I'm running around with a special kind of camera, shouting 'Freeze!' And stay here, right where you are, in this room with me, feeling what you're feeling, and realise that it's not that bad. Realise that you could conceivably feel this, be here, forever.

**Ben**   Look. Why don't we have the deathday party outside? We could go to the bar, or to the park with a black binbag full of alcohol and get wasted and maybe even all fall asleep – well, don't look at me like that, Toper, I think it's a bloody good idea.

**Eve**   Let's have a vote. Who wants to have the deathday party in the bar?

**Ben**'s *hand shoots up immediately, followed by* **Toper**'s. **Eve** *deliberately doesn't look at* **Megan**, *who looks at the others, then back at* **Eve**, *and doesn't put her hand up.*

**Eve**   All right, then. I think that means something else has to be the decider.

**Toper**   Hey, yeah. I have an idea. Show Megan that photo album of yours. If it makes her cry, then we go to the bar.

**Toper** *grabs the photo album from the desk and holds it out of* **Eve**'s *reach in preparation for her to jump at it, but she merely stays where she is, holding her hands out to catch it as if expecting him to throw it to her.* **Megan** *goes towards* **Toper** *but* **Ben** *laconically takes her arm and moves her easily out of* **Toper**'s *way.*

**Megan**   Why would I cry? Let me see it!

**Toper**   I was counting on you not having shown her.

**Ben** *sighs.*

**Ben**   Don't let her see it, Toper. I know you're tired, man, but if you do this . . .

**Eve** (*to no one in particular*)   Listen, I'm not afraid of anything I've done. I'm not afraid of anyone, and especially not you, because all you can do to me is lie, and that doesn't hurt unless I believe you. So if you want to threaten me, good, do it.

**Toper**   Um, I think I already am. Are you leaving this room with us tonight or am I handing this to Megan?

**Megan**   Evie? I wish you'd tell me when something's wrong. I wish . . . oh, what's the point?

*Eve suddenly jumps towards* **Toper**. *He is caught by surprise and steps back, letting the book fall.* **Megan** *grabs it quickly, but* **Ben** *plucks the book from her hands and throws it across the room.* **Eve** *goes into her drawer and comes up with handfuls of paper.*

**Eve**   Hey, Megan, Ben, I thought I might entertain you with some love letters a boy wrote me.

**Toper**   Eve.

*Eve meets his eyes, then looks down again, scrabbling at her papers.*

**Eve**   It's all a bit patchy at the moment, because I was cutting them up the other day, but I'm sure a few sentences will suffice to show you how people create their loves so that they're unreal –

**Ben** *settles down in the chair by the door and assumes an expression of intense interest, looking slowly from* **Eve** *to* **Toper** *and back again.* **Megan** *hovers and then moves to stand behind his chair, biting her nails and watching the situation.*

**Toper**   (*looking at the others to check their reaction to* **Eve**'s *words*) I didn't – don't say that –

**Eve**   I can love, oh yes I can, I can, and I can, and I can, until someone loves me into victimese. Then it stops. He says this: 'I like the vanity of believing you're my craft.' And he says he dreamed me. Ha! Dreamed me!

**Toper** *goes and picks up* **Eve**'s *photo album and stands staring hard at the cover as if he is unable to brace himself to open it.* **Ben** *reclines in the chair, looking at the ground, while* **Megan** *flies across the room and tries to hug* **Eve**.

**Megan**   Evie . . . is that why you were upset? Oh, and your wrists . . .

**Eve**    Upset? I am not upset! I'm waiting. Why can't any of you understand that? You think I'm staying in because I broke up with my frigging boyfriend?

**Megan**    But the bandages – what happened?

**Ben**    Eve? You know what, don't worry. If you really want to, we'll stay in. I don't wanna be taking all this crazy stuff to a public setting. But I've got to get some sleep in between now and tonight, okay? I can't process all this. I mean, I – (*He stops, makes a face, shakes his head.*) Can't remember what I was about to say

**Eve**    It's all right, Ben. Go and get some rest. See? I know what you need. I know that you need approval to do something that will help you. Shall I kick my sympathetic voice up a notch?

**Toper** *and* **Ben** *look across the room at each other,* **Toper** *long-suffering,* **Ben** *trying to hide amusement.*

**Megan**    Why are you being mean to him? He's just agreed to do what you want. I don't even know why he still wants to come!

**Ben**    Eve makes me uncomfortable – she's one of the very few people that do.

**Ben** *stands and goes to the door.* **Toper** *goes towards him, handing the photo album to* **Eve** *as he does so.*

**Toper** (*in a low voice*)    She's out there; go and meet her halfway, because I don't think it's up to you to let her in after all.

**Ben**    We'll be back with drinks. Appoint an hour, and we'll see you then.

**Eve** *sits down on the bed and clutches the photo album, staring stonily ahead of her.* **Megan** *looks at her and decides to fill the silence.*

**Megan**    Um, does ten o'clock sound okay?

**Ben**    Good girl. See you then.

**Toper**    Hey, I'm sorry about this, Megan.

**Megan**    Oh shush, it's not your fault. See you later!

*Exit* **Toper** *and* **Ben**.

**Megan** *joins* **Eve** *on the bed, and* **Eve** *stirs, then blinks rapidly, gets up and stores the photo album in her top desk-drawer. She seems about to say something, then looks at her sister, who is glaring at her, and falls silent.*

**Megan**    You don't want to be made a victim yourself, but you make me tell you everything that's wrong with me. I don't think you know of a single good thing that's happened to me in ages.

**Eve**    Would you like to forgive me?

**Megan**    Yes.

**Eve**    I'm not going to give you the chance. If you want to go out and get food, do it. Just walk out. Why are you letting me make you unhappy?

**Megan**    I think Toper's unhappy too. I think it's because of you as well. Why do you think he's letting you make him unhappy?

**Eve**    Toper is moody because he can't sleep. He said so himself.

**Megan**    Yeah, and people always say what they mean, don't they?

**Eve** *comes and lays her head on* **Megan**'s *lap, and* **Megan**, *startled, freezes for a second, then strokes her hair.*

**Eve**    I'm sorry if I've changed you so you don't like yourself properly. I know . . . that you could have been different.

**Megan**    Different how?

**Eve** (*with difficulty*)    Happier-different.

**Megan** *looks around the room as if fearing to be burst in on, then looks at* **Eve** *again.*

**Megan**   I don't forgive you.

**Megan** *bends her head to kiss* **Eve**'s *forehead.*

*Blackout.*


**Three**

**Eve**, **Megan**, **Toper** *and* **Ben** *are sitting on the floor in a shadowy circle, and in the surrounding candlelight their faces are first almost featureless, then illuminated.* **Ben** *is drinking wine straight from the bottle, and* **Toper** *is lighting the candles (nineteen) on* **Eve**'s *chocolate deathday cake.*

**Eve**, **Megan**, **Toper** *and* **Ben**
   Happy deathday to us,
   Happy deathday to us,
   Happy deathday, dear us . . .
   Happy deathday to us!

**Ben** *puts his bottle down, rubs his head with both hands, then shakes his head hard.*

**Ben**   Weird.

**Megan**   Did you get any sleep, Ben?

**Ben**   No. I got distracted at about eleven a.m. by someone dancing on the lawn in a black cape.

**Eve**   Dan was drunk at eleven a.m.?

**Toper**   Again?

**Ben**   No, I don't think the dancer was real.

**Eve**   Oh dear.

**Megan** *giggles, and* **Eve** *and* **Toper** *look at* **Ben**, *smiling.* **Ben** *lowers his head and knits his brow as he tries to concentrate.*

**Ben**    This is the thing: I got out of bed because I could hear the cape swishing like a chopper. No music. And when I looked out, this dancing person was so small they were an animated comma, leaking swirls of black ink.

**Toper**    Ben –

**Ben** *picks up the wine bottle again and takes a swig out of it.*

**Ben**    Yeah, yeah, I know. Got to get some sleep. But how?

*With* **Megan** *leaning eagerly over her pointing out the bit of the cake that she wants,* **Eve** *turns the cake around towards her and starts to cut it.*

**Eve**    Well, you know, when you die, you can sleep forever. So maybe your body's holding you back from the brink just that little bit longer so the adrenaline of the jump truly bites. Maybe you're getting you ready for the biggest sleep.

**Ben**    Bring it on.

**Eve** *hands* **Ben** *a huge slice of cake on a paper plate, and he takes a big bite of it, then slurps down more wine, leaving a cakey mouthprint around the bottle opening.*

**Toper**    For God's sake, share the wine.

**Ben**    Ah, but I might need it to help me get through the night.

**Toper**    Are you drunk already?

**Ben**    No – how dare you?

**Toper**    Megan, pass me a beer, please.

**Megan** *takes a beer from the six-pack beside her and hands it to* **Toper***, who opens it and starts drinking.*

**Ben** (*to* **Megan**)    You have one too.

**Eve**    I think not.

**Megan**    Eve! I'm not a baby!

**Eve**   Oh please, it's not that. I just don't think I could bear you if you got drunk. I imagine you as a squeaker; your voice getting shriller and shriller as you spiral up the spaghetti-strand rungs of that beer-happiness ladder.

**Ben** (*pointing randomly to the far corner of the room*)   Have a shandy.

**Megan**   Good job, because I actually love shandy.

**Ben**   Very good.

**Megan** *opens a shandy and leans back, resting on one hand, as she swigs it.* **Ben** *and* **Toper** *watch her and the way the liquid pulses down her bared throat.*

**Ben**   Yum-yum.

**Toper** *laughs and* **Megan** *tries to kick him, but* **Eve** *frowns.*

**Eve**   Let's tell secrets.

**Toper**   Okay, you go first.

**Eve**   No, that's not fair, it was my idea, so I should get a rest.

**Toper**   Fine. Ben, you're up first.

**Ben** *takes a reflective swig from his bottle.*

**Ben**   Right. My secret is that I'm scared of my family.

*The others immediately look at him over-attentively, stifling half-spoken murmurs, and* **Ben**'s *gaze singles out* **Megan** *as he drinks some more wine. His stare is overlong, and she is forced to look away.*

**Ben**   Well, scared; what is that? I mean, more scared as in mistrustful. It's just a fear, a creeping, gradual thing like when some random eight-year-old somewhere wakes up and feels their pyjamas sticking wetly to them. The kid will think: have I done it, have I myself? But they won't want to check until the last possible moment, because of the shame. It's like that with me: a thing that I kind of know but I just don't want to get a handle on. The idea of peeling back heavy layers only bothers you because of the stark, shallow, almost pathetic cuts you find underneath.

**Megan**   Do I want to hear this? I don't think I do, you know.

**Ben**   Oh, don't be such a pussy. It's nothing particularly bad – it's not even bad at all. It doesn't give me a motive or a reason for the way I am, nothing like that. All it means is that I try just that little bit harder with my parents; try to make them want to keep me. I'm an only child, you know – if I fuck up, there are no more chances. Shit, the wine's finished. Toper –

**Toper** *silently hands him a can of beer, and* **Ben** *starts on that.*

**Ben**   The worst thing is knowing the exact moment when you realise that you have to be careful, that all love is conditional, that even if someone says they care about you and live for you and think about you all the time, it can't possibly be true. There will be seconds, minutes, half-hours when this person, these people who love you forget that you exist, and even the best intentions in the world can't change that. I can't remember how old I was, but me and my mum were shopping in this enormous supermarket. I was a little bit scared because everything was so unbelievably bright and hard around the edges – this forcefully yellow electricity zinging off everything; the aisles should have been smooth lines that, I don't know, ran away with you into the light or something. But they were bumpy and made irregular by cardboard signs and squeaky-wheeled trolleys; the whole place was trying to look soft, but had a hardness to it underneath – a 'get your frigging groceries and leave, okay' vibe to it. I was confused because each item I passed had become a huge threat – usually it's not a problem pretending not to be scared of things, but you know it's getting silly when you have to conjure up bravado against a packet of rubber gloves.

**Megan** *and* **Eve** *snigger, but* **Toper** *absent-mindedly makes shushing gestures at them. Despite having paused,* **Ben** *doesn't seem to notice that the others have laughed. He takes another sip of beer.*

**Ben**   Anyways, all these rows of canned, boxed, branded normality – they were bigger, and harsher; teeth pulled out

of the context of a smiling mouth. And these trolleys,
clattering and clattering . . . basically, I was very, very keen
to get out, but also very keen not to let my mum know
this. So I made myself leave her while she was looking at
different types of tinned tomato. I let go of her hand, and
when my hand was away from hers, it made me realise just
how clammy it'd got. Then I ran away round a corner and
went stomping down the other aisle in my Caterpillars.
I thought I'd meet her at the end, and I thought I'd prove
to myself that for a couple of seconds I could be alone in
this weirdly lit hell-hole of a supermarket. But when I got
to the end of the next aisle, she hadn't missed me at all.
She had two cans in her hands and was comparing them.
I remember I was really annoyed that she hadn't noticed
I was gone. I wasn't frightened just then, though, because
I had her, I could see her. Then she must have felt me
looking at her, because she turned her head and looked
straight at me – (*He throws his head back and noisily draws in air.*)
Sorry. She looked straight at me, and her face was just . . .
empty. It was swingbin-smooth, like everything that made
me know her had fallen from the top of her skull into some
basement in her chin. Afterwards, she said she hadn't seen
me, but I really don't think I would've gotten as scared as
I did for nothing. She saw me – she looked right at me for
about half a second, really coldly, and then she chose her
can – she put one in the trolley and walked away, pushing
this trolley in front of her, and she left me there. And the
worst thing was that I didn't know why. I don't know
whether it was something in me, or something in her, or
what – my mum is usually the most predictable person ever –
but that moment . . . I don't know.

**Megan**   How did she find you again afterwards?

**Ben**   I stood there for another five minutes or so, just not
believing it, then I went to some girl who was sitting at the
last checkout, and I cried like a bitch until my mother came
running in response to a tannoy they put out for 'Benjamin
Brown's mum'.

**Eve**   I liked that secret. I think you told the truth.

**Ben**   What else would I tell?

**Eve**   I don't know . . . something that covered up how bloody scared you were just for that second. Something that made it up to us to make you better.

**Ben**   Make me better.

**Eve**   What? Aren't we still here, looking at you? Isn't that enough?

**Ben**   Is it your turn now?

**Toper** *and* **Megan** *turn their heads attentively away from the cake they are eating, and* **Ben** *shakes his can to test the remaining beer level and then takes a swig.*

**Eve**   It's a very simple secret; the only point in telling it is that none of you know for sure, though you may have your own suspicions. It's the reason why I started cutting myself.

**Megan** *winces and fumbles for* **Eve**'s *hand, but* **Eve** *pats her hand and then puts it back in her lap.*

**Eve**   Our parents believe that crying is silly.

**Megan** *nods emphatically at the others, horror on her face at the thought of crying in front of her family.*

**Eve**   If you cry over something, you are wasting time and emotion. You are making things inconvenient for other people. So I've kind of come to hate crying. I'm just . . . instantly annoyed when people start doing it. It's like deep inside I know that tears aren't just water, that they mean something, but the feeling's too far beneath to affect the way I react to them. People who cry are people who are wrong, people who have been found out, people who allow themselves to be hurt.

**Toper**   You realise that you cried when you read my first letter?

**Eve**   Yes, by accident. If I'd've seen it coming, I . . . well, there was no way of seeing it coming, I suppose.

**Toper**   What did you do?

**Eve**   I couldn't understand it. For a long time, I'd been schooling myself so I didn't cry over things. Unfortunately for me, I used to cry very easily – I don't know if I have some kind of inbuilt melancholy trigger, but for ages I'd have to run away and cry despite, or maybe because of, nothing being wrong. But I learnt to pull myself together. I tested myself against things to see if I'd cry – I got to a point where I could dip my index finger up to the knuckle in hot oil and only say 'Shit'.

**Ben**   Indeed. The water is getting deep.

**Ben** *gets up and goes across to* **Eve***'s bed, pulling off his shoes before climbing in and turning over so that his back is to the other three.*

**Megan**   When was this?

**Eve**   I was about fifteen. That'd make you twelve.

**Megan**   Where was I?

**Eve**   I don't know, Megan. I really didn't used to think about you that much, if you want the truth.

**Megan**   I know you didn't. I know you don't. Why do you think I keep on coming to you with all these problems?

**Eve**   Megan –

**Megan** *leans right into* **Eve***'s face and speaks in a loud whisper.*

**Megan**   It's so you'll remember me – even if it only worries or annoys you to know I'm alive, I have to make sure you think about me sometimes.

**Toper** *touches* **Megan***'s arm to calm her, and* **Megan** *leans back, holding on to his hand.*

**Eve**   I've already said I'm sorry. I have a catalogue of sorrys I've said for crying, and I don't want you to see them,

Megan, because you'll misunderstand, and you'll think that I need your help, when actually all I need is for that girl, that woman, who is coming to see me, to hurry up and come.

**Ben** *sits up in bed, listening, but none of the others notice that he has woken up.*

**Toper**    Tell us the rest.

**Eve**    Yeah, so I was at a stage where if I wanted to cry, I could bypass it completely by zoning in on all the physical pain that had happened to me before.

**Toper**    That you had inflicted on yourself, you mean –

**Eve**    That had happened to me before. When I came here, I suppose I was semi-prepared, but I wasn't ready enough for someone to tell me the things that you wanted to tell me. I – it hurt so much reading your letters that – how weird is this? I felt as if all the tears I hadn't cried were pouring out. It wasn't a normal reaction to a love letter, I know, but. But. I was scared that I might end up crying for days, and I wanted all that water to fall out of me, quickly, quickly, because it felt so bad. I think I wanted to fall out of my skin. I don't actually know if I can pin cutting so deep along here and here – (*She indicates.*) to a rational thing. I bled, and I didn't feel better, and I was still crying, and –

**Megan** (*almost at the same time as* **Toper** *speaks*)    Eve, I almost hate you for this.

**Toper**    You did it to yourself.

**Eve**    How could I have? It hurt the first time, and I didn't like it, but it kept on happening. It wasn't me.

**Ben**    'It wasn't me.' Who the hell was it, then? That's the first time I ever heard you sound like a victim. Someone else is responsible for your pain, are they?

**Eve** (*voice rising in pitch*)    You – you do not know me anywhere near well enough to tell me when I'm not taking responsibility –

**Ben**   Deal with it, Eve. Fucking deal with it. You have the most incredible aim, because you are shitting on everyone else at the same time as shitting very heavily on yourself.

**Eve**   You don't know anything. You don't know what it's been like –

**Ben** (*gently, like teacher mildly reproving pupil*)   Worse and worse! Didn't you say you felt as if you were in a school for victimese? You're getting better at it.

**Eve** *sharply swings her head around and looks away from him, silent.*
**Toper** *looks at them both and self-consciously stretches and yawns.*

**Toper**   Um. I'm actually getting sleepy.

**Ben**   I'm not. Never been wider awake. Let's talk some more. I was thinking, Eve, that you need to touch bottom – just so you know you can do it. So you know it's not that difficult; so you know that you don't have to tunnel far; so you know that you're not actually as deep as you think you are. Do it. Have a breakdown. I have never been more serious; be sure and have a breakdown, won't you?

**Eve** *sticks her middle finger up, looks at it in fake surprise and turns it to face* **Ben**.

**Eve**   Wow, look at this.

**Ben** (*to* **Megan** *and* **Toper**)   Shall we take a walk? Let's all take a walk and leave her with a hob and a saucepan full of hot oil. Hours of fun.

**Toper**   Guys, let's take a walk. This is officially cabin fever.

*No one listens to him.* **Megan** *looks as if she is about to rise to* **Ben***'s comment, but turns and speaks to* **Eve** *instead, and* **Ben** *gives an 'I tried' shrug and settles down again.*

**Megan**   Evie, listen to me – I think it's a bit like Ben said, maybe. Maybe if you just cry and cry and cry, you'll wear . . . this disgust thing . . . right out. When I think 'touching bottom', I think it means you need to take a deep breath and dive, and place your hand on your own sea-bed so it's like a concrete starfish that holds both parts of you together.

**Eve** *is clearly not listening, and her reply is stiff and oddly formalised.*

**Eve**    Thank you. Perhaps you're right. I'll think about that.

**Megan** *(very quickly, as if afraid that she might want to snatch the words back)*    My secret is this: I heard you crying in your room when I was having my eighth birthday party. And I knew that something was wrong, and that you'd never tell me, and I was so angry with you that I tore your history homework into pieces and threw it away. And you didn't notice until the night before it was due, and thought you'd lost it, and you sat at the kitchen table for ages, looking up your references all over again. I remember your finger was wobbling across the page because you were that tired. I was glad. I was watching you from the stairs.

**Eve**    Well, I don't remember that.

**Megan** *sways backwards as she flinches, and* **Toper** *looks, astonished, at the anger on her face.* **Ben** *climbs out of bed and creeps up to* **Megan**, *putting his hands on her shoulders to surround her and hold her steady.*

**Megan**    I didn't think you would. You probably don't remember why you were crying, either. You'd organised a birthday party for me and Susie and the others, but you wouldn't come to the party yourself, even though I'd written you out an invitation. I felt like crying all through that stupid party. When I got some jelly off the spoon and into my mouth, the fatness of it made me want to scream. We were all playing musical chairs and pass-the-parcel in the sitting room, and Mummy was in bed with a headache because she didn't want anything to do with it, and when I went up to try and persuade you to come down, you were sobbing so hard I was frightened. I could hear you fighting for breath through the door. Why do you hurt so much, Eve, and not share it?

**Eve**    I suppose I have to keep it all for her.

**Megan**    What about me? Where am I? Tell me where I am and that's where I'll be. Really, I promise. How can I love you and you not care at all?

**Eve** *stays perfectly still and looks impassively at* **Megan** *as* **Ben** *hugs* **Megan***, rocking her backwards and forwards with the strength of his embrace.* **Toper** *watches, with his legs crossed, chin in hand, his gaze on* **Eve***.*

**Megan**    I just don't know what I have to do –

**Ben**    Shush, shush.

**Toper** (*to* **Eve**)    Well, you know what my 'secret' is. It's not really a secret. You know the letters aren't lies, don't you?

**Eve**    Go to bed. Everybody; I mean. Everybody just go to bed. Go to sleep. If you like, I'll make you a special promise; that everything will be all right in the morning.

**Megan**    I forgive you. I really do, Eve, seriously, I do.

**Eve**    Okay.

**Toper**    Eve –

**Megan**    Okay?

**Eve**    There's nothing I can say to you to convince you that I have feeling; it's gotten so everything you say to me is pre-muted; like you don't expect to be heard.

**Ben** *takes* **Megan** *by the hand and helps her up.*

**Ben**    Have the bed.

**Megan** *starts to protest, but* **Ben** *bustles her into bed and tucks her in.* **Ben** *goes over and takes his pillow and blanket out from the corner and arranges it next to the bed so that he can lie on it.*

**Megan** (*laughs tiredly*)    Where's Eve going to sleep? Eve, I'm sorry, I've stolen the bed –

**Ben** (*to* **Toper**)    Will you settle for the floor or risk sharing my bedspace?

**Toper**    Floor.

**Eve** *begins to leave the room, but* **Megan** *sits up and puts her hands out.*

**Megan**    You're going to run away. Where are you going?

**Toper** *half-raises his arm to let Megan know that somehow he will try to handle things, and follows* **Eve** *to the door.* **Megan** *half-heartedly tries to get up, but* **Ben** *contains her easily – she lies back down because she is avoiding his touch.*

**Ben**    She'll be back in a minute.

**Megan**    Yeah, in a minute, and no doubt she'll be crying, and she'll ask me for a hug.

*She smiles unhappily and tucks herself up again, watching* **Toper** *and* **Eve***, though pretending not to.*

**Toper**    Tell me why I'm scared for you.

**Eve**    Because you know she's really there. Maybe she won't hurt me. Maybe we'll just talk about things and work it out so that I can be all right again.

**Toper** (*short laugh*)    Talk about things? With a fiction – with someone incidentally beautiful, and purposefully cruel? Do you actually believe that?

**Eve**    Nope.

**Eve** *tips her head and looks at him, smiling nervously as he takes her in unsmiling.*

*Exit* **Eve**. *All three look at each other and wait a second, then, within seconds of each other, rise, reach for their kicked-off shoes to follow her, appear to change their minds, and leave them.*

*Fade to black.*

9 780413 774781